This Log Belongs to

_____

Mileage Log Book

Employee ID :- _____ Name:- _____

Title :-_____ Dept:- _____

Vehicle Id _____ Signature:-_____

Date:	Time
Purpose:-	
Location - Origin	Destination
Odometer start	Odometer Finish
Gas fill up :- Yes/No	If yes Gallons filled
Cost per gallon	Amount paid
Paid Parking:-	Paid Tolls:-

Date:	Time
Purpose:-	
Location - Origin	Destination
Odometer start	Odometer Finish
Gas fill up :- Yes/No	If yes Gallons filled
Cost per gallon	Amount paid
Paid Parking:-	Paid Tolls:-

Mileage Log Book

Employee ID :- _____ Name:- _____

Title :-_____ Dept:- _____

Vehicle Id _____ Signature:-_____

Date: Time

Purpose:-

Location - Origin	Destination
Odometer start	Odometer Finish
Gas fill up :- Yes/No	If yes Gallons filled
Cost per gallon	Amount paid
Paid Parking:-	Paid Tolls:-

Date: Time

Purpose:-

Location - Origin	Destination
Odometer start	Odometer Finish
Gas fill up :- Yes/No	If yes Gallons filled
Cost per gallon	Amount paid
Paid Parking:-	Paid Tolls:-

Mileage Log Book

Employee ID :- _____ Name:- _____

Title :-_____ Dept:- _____

Vehicle Id _____ Signature:-_____

Date:	Time
Purpose:-	
Location - Origin	Destination
Odometer start	Odometer Finish
Gas fill up :- Yes/No	If yes Gallons filled
Cost per gallon	Amount paid
Paid Parking:-	Paid Tolls:-
Date:	Time
Purpose:-	
Location - Origin	Destination
Odometer start	Odometer Finish
Gas fill up :- Yes/No	If yes Gallons filled
Cost per gallon	Amount paid
Paid Parking:-	Paid Tolls:-

Mileage Log Book

Employee ID :- _____ Name:- _____

Title :-_____ Dept:- _____

Vehicle Id _____ Signature:-_____

Date: Time

Purpose:-

Location - Origin   Destination

Odometer start   Odometer Finish

Gas fill up :- Yes/No   If yes Gallons filled

Cost per gallon   Amount paid

Paid Parking:-   Paid Tolls:-

Date: Time

Purpose:-

Location - Origin   Destination

Odometer start   Odometer Finish

Gas fill up :- Yes/No   If yes Gallons filled

Cost per gallon   Amount paid

Paid Parking:-   Paid Tolls:-

Mileage Log Book

Employee ID :- _____ Name:- _____

Title :-_____ Dept:- _____

Vehicle Id _____ Signature:-_____

Date:	Time
Purpose:-	
Location - Origin	Destination
Odometer start	Odometer Finish
Gas fill up :- Yes/No	If yes Gallons filled
Cost per gallon	Amount paid
Paid Parking:-	Paid Tolls:-

Date:	Time
Purpose:-	
Location - Origin	Destination
Odometer start	Odometer Finish
Gas fill up :- Yes/No	If yes Gallons filled
Cost per gallon	Amount paid
Paid Parking:-	Paid Tolls:-

Mileage Log Book

Employee ID :- _____ Name:- _____

Title :-_____ Dept:- _____

Vehicle Id _____ Signature:-_____

Date: Time

Purpose:-

Location - Origin   Destination

Odometer start   Odometer Finish

Gas fill up :- Yes/No   If yes Gallons filled

Cost per gallon   Amount paid

Paid Parking:-   Paid Tolls:-

Date: Time

Purpose:-

Location - Origin   Destination

Odometer start   Odometer Finish

Gas fill up :- Yes/No   If yes Gallons filled

Cost per gallon   Amount paid

Paid Parking:-   Paid Tolls:-

Mileage Log Book

Employee ID :- _____ Name:- _____

Title :-_____ Dept:- _____

Vehicle Id _____ Signature:-_____

Date: Time

Purpose:-

Location - Origin	Destination
Odometer start	Odometer Finish
Gas fill up :- Yes/No	If yes Gallons filled
Cost per gallon	Amount paid
Paid Parking:-	Paid Tolls:-

Date: Time

Purpose:-

Location - Origin	Destination
Odometer start	Odometer Finish
Gas fill up :- Yes/No	If yes Gallons filled
Cost per gallon	Amount paid
Paid Parking:-	Paid Tolls:-

Mileage Log Book

Employee ID :- _____ Name:- _____

Title :-_____ Dept:- _____

Vehicle Id _____ Signature:-_____

Date:	Time
Purpose:-	
Location - Origin	Destination
Odometer start	Odometer Finish
Gas fill up :- Yes/No	If yes Gallons filled
Cost per gallon	Amount paid
Paid Parking:-	Paid Tolls:-

Date:	Time
Purpose:-	
Location - Origin	Destination
Odometer start	Odometer Finish
Gas fill up :- Yes/No	If yes Gallons filled
Cost per gallon	Amount paid
Paid Parking:-	Paid Tolls:-

Mileage Log Book

Employee ID :- _____ Name:- _____

Title :-_____ Dept:- _____

Vehicle Id _____ Signature:-_____

Date: Time

Purpose:-

Location - Origin	Destination
Odometer start	Odometer Finish
Gas fill up :- Yes/No	If yes Gallons filled
Cost per gallon	Amount paid
Paid Parking:-	Paid Tolls:-

Date: Time

Purpose:-

Location - Origin	Destination
Odometer start	Odometer Finish
Gas fill up :- Yes/No	If yes Gallons filled
Cost per gallon	Amount paid
Paid Parking:-	Paid Tolls:-

Mileage Log Book

Employee ID :- _____ Name:- _____

Title :-_____ Dept:- _____

Vehicle Id _____ Signature:-_____

Date: _____ Time _____

Purpose:-

Location - Origin	Destination
Odometer start	Odometer Finish
Gas fill up :- Yes/No	If yes Gallons filled
Cost per gallon	Amount paid
Paid Parking:-	Paid Tolls:-

Date: _____ Time _____

Purpose:-

Location - Origin	Destination
Odometer start	Odometer Finish
Gas fill up :- Yes/No	If yes Gallons filled
Cost per gallon	Amount paid
Paid Parking:-	Paid Tolls:-

Mileage Log Book

Employee ID :- _____ Name:- _____

Title :-_____ Dept:- _____

Vehicle Id _____ Signature:-_____

Date:	Time
Purpose:-	
Location - Origin	Destination
Odometer start	Odometer Finish
Gas fill up :- Yes/No	If yes Gallons filled
Cost per gallon	Amount paid
Paid Parking:-	Paid Tolls:-

Date:	Time
Purpose:-	
Location - Origin	Destination
Odometer start	Odometer Finish
Gas fill up :- Yes/No	If yes Gallons filled
Cost per gallon	Amount paid
Paid Parking:-	Paid Tolls:-

Mileage Log Book

Employee ID :- _____ Name:- _____

Title :-_____ Dept:- _____

Vehicle Id _____ Signature:-_____

Date:	Time
Purpose:-	
Location - Origin	Destination
Odometer start	Odometer Finish
Gas fill up :- Yes/No	If yes Gallons filled
Cost per gallon	Amount paid
Paid Parking:-	Paid Tolls:-

Date:	Time
Purpose:-	
Location - Origin	Destination
Odometer start	Odometer Finish
Gas fill up :- Yes/No	If yes Gallons filled
Cost per gallon	Amount paid
Paid Parking:-	Paid Tolls:-

Mileage Log Book

Employee ID :- _____ Name:- _____

Title :-_____ Dept:- _____

Vehicle Id _____ Signature:-_____

Date:	Time
Purpose:-	
Location - Origin	Destination
Odometer start	Odometer Finish
Gas fill up :- Yes/No	If yes Gallons filled
Cost per gallon	Amount paid
Paid Parking:-	Paid Tolls:-

Date:	Time
Purpose:-	
Location - Origin	Destination
Odometer start	Odometer Finish
Gas fill up :- Yes/No	If yes Gallons filled
Cost per gallon	Amount paid
Paid Parking:-	Paid Tolls:-

Mileage Log Book

Employee ID :- _____ Name:- _____

Title :-_____ Dept:- _____

Vehicle Id _____ Signature:-_____

Date:	Time
Purpose:-	
Location - Origin	Destination
Odometer start	Odometer Finish
Gas fill up :- Yes/No	If yes Gallons filled
Cost per gallon	Amount paid
Paid Parking:-	Paid Tolls:-

Date:	Time
Purpose:-	
Location - Origin	Destination
Odometer start	Odometer Finish
Gas fill up :- Yes/No	If yes Gallons filled
Cost per gallon	Amount paid
Paid Parking:-	Paid Tolls:-

Mileage Log Book

Employee ID :- _____ Name:- _____

Title :-_____ Dept:- _____

Vehicle Id _____ Signature:-_____

Date: Time

Purpose:-

Location - Origin	Destination
Odometer start	Odometer Finish
Gas fill up :- Yes/No	If yes Gallons filled
Cost per gallon	Amount paid
Paid Parking:-	Paid Tolls:-

Date: Time

Purpose:-

Location - Origin	Destination
Odometer start	Odometer Finish
Gas fill up :- Yes/No	If yes Gallons filled
Cost per gallon	Amount paid
Paid Parking:-	Paid Tolls:-

Mileage Log Book

Employee ID :- _____ Name:- _____

Title :-_____ Dept:- _____

Vehicle Id _____ Signature:-_____

Date:	Time
Purpose:-	
Location - Origin	Destination
Odometer start	Odometer Finish
Gas fill up :- Yes/No	If yes Gallons filled
Cost per gallon	Amount paid
Paid Parking:-	Paid Tolls:-

Date:	Time
Purpose:-	
Location - Origin	Destination
Odometer start	Odometer Finish
Gas fill up :- Yes/No	If yes Gallons filled
Cost per gallon	Amount paid
Paid Parking:-	Paid Tolls:-

Mileage Log Book

Employee ID :- _____ Name:- _____

Title :-_____ Dept:- _____

Vehicle Id _____ Signature:-_____

Date:	Time
Purpose:-	
Location - Origin	Destination
Odometer start	Odometer Finish
Gas fill up :- Yes/No	If yes Gallons filled
Cost per gallon	Amount paid
Paid Parking:-	Paid Tolls:-

Date:	Time
Purpose:-	
Location - Origin	Destination
Odometer start	Odometer Finish
Gas fill up :- Yes/No	If yes Gallons filled
Cost per gallon	Amount paid
Paid Parking:-	Paid Tolls:-

Mileage Log Book

Employee ID :- _____ Name:- _____

Title :-_____ Dept:- _____

Vehicle Id _____ Signature:-_____

Date:	Time
Purpose:-	
Location - Origin	Destination
Odometer start	Odometer Finish
Gas fill up :- Yes/No	If yes Gallons filled
Cost per gallon	Amount paid
Paid Parking:-	Paid Tolls:-

Date:	Time
Purpose:-	
Location - Origin	Destination
Odometer start	Odometer Finish
Gas fill up :- Yes/No	If yes Gallons filled
Cost per gallon	Amount paid
Paid Parking:-	Paid Tolls:-

Mileage Log Book

Employee ID :- _____ Name:- _____

Title :-_____ Dept:- _____

Vehicle Id _____ Signature:-_____

Date:	Time
Purpose:-	
Location - Origin	Destination
Odometer start	Odometer Finish
Gas fill up :- Yes/No	If yes Gallons filled
Cost per gallon	Amount paid
Paid Parking:-	Paid Tolls:-

Date:	Time
Purpose:-	
Location - Origin	Destination
Odometer start	Odometer Finish
Gas fill up :- Yes/No	If yes Gallons filled
Cost per gallon	Amount paid
Paid Parking:-	Paid Tolls:-

Mileage Log Book

Employee ID :- _____ Name:- _____

Title :-_____ Dept:- _____

Vehicle Id _____ Signature:-_____

Date: _____ Time _____

Purpose:- _____

Location - Origin	Destination
Odometer start	Odometer Finish
Gas fill up :- Yes/No	If yes Gallons filled
Cost per gallon	Amount paid
Paid Parking:-	Paid Tolls:-

- -

Date: _____ Time _____

Purpose:- _____

Location - Origin	Destination
Odometer start	Odometer Finish
Gas fill up :- Yes/No	If yes Gallons filled
Cost per gallon	Amount paid
Paid Parking:-	Paid Tolls:-

Mileage Log Book

Employee ID :- _____ Name:- _____

Title :- _____ Dept:- _____

Vehicle Id _____ Signature:- _____

Date: _____ Time _____

Purpose:-

Location - Origin	Destination
Odometer start	Odometer Finish
Gas fill up :- Yes/No	If yes Gallons filled
Cost per gallon	Amount paid
Paid Parking:-	Paid Tolls:-

Date: _____ Time _____

Purpose:-

Location - Origin	Destination
Odometer start	Odometer Finish
Gas fill up :- Yes/No	If yes Gallons filled
Cost per gallon	Amount paid
Paid Parking:-	Paid Tolls:-

Mileage Log Book

Employee ID :- _____ Name:- _____

Title :- _____ Dept:- _____

Vehicle Id _____ Signature:- _____

Date: Time

Purpose:-

Location - Origin   Destination

Odometer start   Odometer Finish

Gas fill up :- Yes/No   If yes Gallons filled

Cost per gallon   Amount paid

Paid Parking:-   Paid Tolls:-

- -

Date: Time

Purpose:-

Location - Origin   Destination

Odometer start   Odometer Finish

Gas fill up :- Yes/No   If yes Gallons filled

Cost per gallon   Amount paid

Paid Parking:-   Paid Tolls:-

Mileage Log Book

Employee ID :- _____ Name:- _____

Title :-_____ Dept:- _____

Vehicle Id _____ Signature:-_____

Date:	Time
Purpose:-	
Location - Origin	Destination
Odometer start	Odometer Finish
Gas fill up :- Yes/No	If yes Gallons filled
Cost per gallon	Amount paid
Paid Parking:-	Paid Tolls:-
Date:	Time
Purpose:-	
Location - Origin	Destination
Odometer start	Odometer Finish
Gas fill up :- Yes/No	If yes Gallons filled
Cost per gallon	Amount paid
Paid Parking:-	Paid Tolls:-

Mileage Log Book

Employee ID :- _____ Name:- _____

Title :-_____ Dept:- _____

Vehicle Id _____ Signature:-_____

Date: Time

Purpose:-

Location - Origin   Destination

Odometer start   Odometer Finish

Gas fill up :- Yes/No   If yes Gallons filled

Cost per gallon   Amount paid

Paid Parking:-   Paid Tolls:-

Date: Time

Purpose:-

Location - Origin   Destination

Odometer start   Odometer Finish

Gas fill up :- Yes/No   If yes Gallons filled

Cost per gallon   Amount paid

Paid Parking:-   Paid Tolls:-

Mileage Log Book

Employee ID :- _____ Name:- _____

Title :-_____ Dept:- _____

Vehicle Id _____ Signature:-_____

Date:	Time
Purpose:-	
Location - Origin	Destination
Odometer start	Odometer Finish
Gas fill up :- Yes/No	If yes Gallons filled
Cost per gallon	Amount paid
Paid Parking:-	Paid Tolls:-

Date:	Time
Purpose:-	
Location - Origin	Destination
Odometer start	Odometer Finish
Gas fill up :- Yes/No	If yes Gallons filled
Cost per gallon	Amount paid
Paid Parking:-	Paid Tolls:-

Mileage Log Book

Employee ID :- _____ Name:- _____

Title :-_____ Dept:- _____

Vehicle Id _____ Signature:-_____

Date: Time

Purpose:-

Location - Origin	Destination
Odometer start	Odometer Finish
Gas fill up :- Yes/No	If yes Gallons filled
Cost per gallon	Amount paid
Paid Parking:-	Paid Tolls:-

Date: Time

Purpose:-

Location - Origin	Destination
Odometer start	Odometer Finish
Gas fill up :- Yes/No	If yes Gallons filled
Cost per gallon	Amount paid
Paid Parking:-	Paid Tolls:-

Mileage Log Book

Employee ID :- _____ Name:- _____

Title :-_____ Dept:- _____

Vehicle Id _____ Signature:-_____

Date:	Time
Purpose:-	
Location - Origin	Destination
Odometer start	Odometer Finish
Gas fill up :- Yes/No	If yes Gallons filled
Cost per gallon	Amount paid
Paid Parking:-	Paid Tolls:-
Date:	Time
Purpose:-	
Location - Origin	Destination
Odometer start	Odometer Finish
Gas fill up :- Yes/No	If yes Gallons filled
Cost per gallon	Amount paid
Paid Parking:-	Paid Tolls:-

Mileage Log Book

Employee ID :- _____ Name:- _____

Title :-_____ Dept:- _____

Vehicle Id _____ Signature:-_____

Date:	Time
Purpose:-	
Location - Origin	Destination
Odometer start	Odometer Finish
Gas fill up :- Yes/No	If yes Gallons filled
Cost per gallon	Amount paid
Paid Parking:-	Paid Tolls:-

Date:	Time
Purpose:-	
Location - Origin	Destination
Odometer start	Odometer Finish
Gas fill up :- Yes/No	If yes Gallons filled
Cost per gallon	Amount paid
Paid Parking:-	Paid Tolls:-

Mileage Log Book

Employee ID :- _____ Name:- _____

Title :-_____ Dept:- _____

Vehicle Id _____ Signature:-_____

Date:	Time
Purpose:-	
Location - Origin	Destination
Odometer start	Odometer Finish
Gas fill up :- Yes/No	If yes Gallons filled
Cost per gallon	Amount paid
Paid Parking:-	Paid Tolls:-

Date:	Time
Purpose:-	
Location - Origin	Destination
Odometer start	Odometer Finish
Gas fill up :- Yes/No	If yes Gallons filled
Cost per gallon	Amount paid
Paid Parking:-	Paid Tolls:-

Mileage Log Book

Employee ID :- _____ Name:- _____

Title :-_____ Dept:- _____

Vehicle Id _____ Signature:-_____

Date:	Time
Purpose:-	
Location - Origin	Destination
Odometer start	Odometer Finish
Gas fill up :- Yes/No	If yes Gallons filled
Cost per gallon	Amount paid
Paid Parking:-	Paid Tolls:-

Date:	Time
Purpose:-	
Location - Origin	Destination
Odometer start	Odometer Finish
Gas fill up :- Yes/No	If yes Gallons filled
Cost per gallon	Amount paid
Paid Parking:-	Paid Tolls:-

Mileage Log Book

Employee ID :- _____ Name:- _____

Title :-_____ Dept:- _____

Vehicle Id _____ Signature:-_____

Date: Time

Purpose:-

Location - Origin	Destination
Odometer start	Odometer Finish
Gas fill up :- Yes/No	If yes Gallons filled
Cost per gallon	Amount paid
Paid Parking:-	Paid Tolls:-

Date: Time

Purpose:-

Location - Origin	Destination
Odometer start	Odometer Finish
Gas fill up :- Yes/No	If yes Gallons filled
Cost per gallon	Amount paid
Paid Parking:-	Paid Tolls:-

Mileage Log Book

Employee ID :- _____ Name:- _____

Title :-_____ Dept:- _____

Vehicle Id _____ Signature:-_____

Date:	Time
Purpose:-	
Location - Origin	Destination
Odometer start	Odometer Finish
Gas fill up :- Yes/No	If yes Gallons filled
Cost per gallon	Amount paid
Paid Parking:-	Paid Tolls:-

Date:	Time
Purpose:-	
Location - Origin	Destination
Odometer start	Odometer Finish
Gas fill up :- Yes/No	If yes Gallons filled
Cost per gallon	Amount paid
Paid Parking:-	Paid Tolls:-

Mileage Log Book

Employee ID :- _____ Name:- _____

Title :-_____ Dept:- _____

Vehicle Id _____ Signature:-_____

Date:	Time
Purpose:-	
Location - Origin	Destination
Odometer start	Odometer Finish
Gas fill up :- Yes/No	If yes Gallons filled
Cost per gallon	Amount paid
Paid Parking:-	Paid Tolls:-

- -

Date:	Time
Purpose:-	
Location - Origin	Destination
Odometer start	Odometer Finish
Gas fill up :- Yes/No	If yes Gallons filled
Cost per gallon	Amount paid
Paid Parking:-	Paid Tolls:-

Mileage Log Book

Employee ID :- _____ Name:- _____

Title :-_____ Dept:- _____

Vehicle Id _____ Signature:-_____

Date: Time

Purpose:-

Location - Origin   Destination

Odometer start   Odometer Finish

Gas fill up :- Yes/No   If yes Gallons filled

Cost per gallon   Amount paid

Paid Parking:-   Paid Tolls:-

Date: Time

Purpose:-

Location - Origin   Destination

Odometer start   Odometer Finish

Gas fill up :- Yes/No   If yes Gallons filled

Cost per gallon   Amount paid

Paid Parking:-   Paid Tolls:-

Mileage Log Book

Employee ID :- _____ Name:- _____

Title :- _____ Dept:- _____

Vehicle Id _____ Signature:- _____

Date:	Time
Purpose:-	
Location - Origin	Destination
Odometer start	Odometer Finish
Gas fill up :- Yes/No	If yes Gallons filled
Cost per gallon	Amount paid
Paid Parking:-	Paid Tolls:-

Date:	Time
Purpose:-	
Location - Origin	Destination
Odometer start	Odometer Finish
Gas fill up :- Yes/No	If yes Gallons filled
Cost per gallon	Amount paid
Paid Parking:-	Paid Tolls:-

Mileage Log Book

Employee ID :- _____ Name:- _____

Title :-_____ Dept:- _____

Vehicle Id _____ Signature:-_____

Date: Time

Purpose:-

Location - Origin   Destination

Odometer start   Odometer Finish

Gas fill up :- Yes/No   If yes Gallons filled

Cost per gallon   Amount paid

Paid Parking:-   Paid Tolls:-

- -

Date: Time

Purpose:-

Location - Origin   Destination

Odometer start   Odometer Finish

Gas fill up :- Yes/No   If yes Gallons filled

Cost per gallon   Amount paid

Paid Parking:-   Paid Tolls:-

Mileage Log Book

Employee ID :- _____ Name:- _____

Title :-_____ Dept:- _____

Vehicle Id _____ Signature:-_____

Date:	Time
Purpose:-	
Location - Origin	Destination
Odometer start	Odometer Finish
Gas fill up :- Yes/No	If yes Gallons filled
Cost per gallon	Amount paid
Paid Parking:-	Paid Tolls:-

Date:	Time
Purpose:-	
Location - Origin	Destination
Odometer start	Odometer Finish
Gas fill up :- Yes/No	If yes Gallons filled
Cost per gallon	Amount paid
Paid Parking:-	Paid Tolls:-

Mileage Log Book

Employee ID :- _____ Name:- _____

Title :-_____ Dept:- _____

Vehicle Id _____ Signature:-_____

Date:	Time
Purpose:-	
Location - Origin	Destination
Odometer start	Odometer Finish
Gas fill up :- Yes/No	If yes Gallons filled
Cost per gallon	Amount paid
Paid Parking:-	Paid Tolls:-

Date:	Time
Purpose:-	
Location - Origin	Destination
Odometer start	Odometer Finish
Gas fill up :- Yes/No	If yes Gallons filled
Cost per gallon	Amount paid
Paid Parking:-	Paid Tolls:-

Mileage Log Book

Employee ID :- _____ Name:- _____

Title :-_____ Dept:- _____

Vehicle Id _____ Signature:-_____

Date: Time

Purpose:-

Location - Origin   Destination

Odometer start   Odometer Finish

Gas fill up :- Yes/No   If yes Gallons filled

Cost per gallon   Amount paid

Paid Parking:-   Paid Tolls:-

Date: Time

Purpose:-

Location - Origin   Destination

Odometer start   Odometer Finish

Gas fill up :- Yes/No   If yes Gallons filled

Cost per gallon   Amount paid

Paid Parking:-   Paid Tolls:-

Mileage Log Book

Employee ID :- _____ Name:- _____

Title :-_____ Dept:- _____

Vehicle Id _____ Signature:-_____

Date: Time

Purpose:-

Location - Origin	Destination
Odometer start	Odometer Finish
Gas fill up :- Yes/No	If yes Gallons filled
Cost per gallon	Amount paid
Paid Parking:-	Paid Tolls:-

Date: Time

Purpose:-

Location - Origin	Destination
Odometer start	Odometer Finish
Gas fill up :- Yes/No	If yes Gallons filled
Cost per gallon	Amount paid
Paid Parking:-	Paid Tolls:-

Mileage Log Book

Employee ID :- _____ Name:- _____

Title :-_____ Dept:- _____

Vehicle Id _____ Signature:-_____

Date:	Time
Purpose:-	
Location - Origin	Destination
Odometer start	Odometer Finish
Gas fill up :- Yes/No	If yes Gallons filled
Cost per gallon	Amount paid
Paid Parking:-	Paid Tolls:-
Date:	Time
Purpose:-	
Location - Origin	Destination
Odometer start	Odometer Finish
Gas fill up :- Yes/No	If yes Gallons filled
Cost per gallon	Amount paid
Paid Parking:-	Paid Tolls:-

Mileage Log Book

Employee ID :- _____ Name:- _____

Title :-_____ Dept:- _____

Vehicle Id _____ Signature:-_____

Date: Time

Purpose:-

Location - Origin	Destination
Odometer start	Odometer Finish
Gas fill up :- Yes/No	If yes Gallons filled
Cost per gallon	Amount paid
Paid Parking:-	Paid Tolls:-

Date: Time

Purpose:-

Location - Origin	Destination
Odometer start	Odometer Finish
Gas fill up :- Yes/No	If yes Gallons filled
Cost per gallon	Amount paid
Paid Parking:-	Paid Tolls:-

Mileage Log Book

Employee ID :- _____ Name:- _____

Title :-_____ Dept:- _____

Vehicle Id _____ Signature:-_____

Date: Time

Purpose:-

Location - Origin   Destination

Odometer start   Odometer Finish

Gas fill up :- Yes/No   If yes Gallons filled

Cost per gallon   Amount paid

Paid Parking:-   Paid Tolls:-

Date: Time

Purpose:-

Location - Origin   Destination

Odometer start   Odometer Finish

Gas fill up :- Yes/No   If yes Gallons filled

Cost per gallon   Amount paid

Paid Parking:-   Paid Tolls:-

Mileage Log Book

Employee ID :- _____ Name:- _____

Title :-_____ Dept:- _____

Vehicle Id _____ Signature:-_____

Date: Time

Purpose:-

Location - Origin   Destination

Odometer start   Odometer Finish

Gas fill up :- Yes/No   If yes Gallons filled

Cost per gallon   Amount paid

Paid Parking:-   Paid Tolls:-

Date: Time

Purpose:-

Location - Origin   Destination

Odometer start   Odometer Finish

Gas fill up :- Yes/No   If yes Gallons filled

Cost per gallon   Amount paid

Paid Parking:-   Paid Tolls:-

Mileage Log Book

Employee ID :- _____ Name:- _____

Title :-_____ Dept:- _____

Vehicle Id _____ Signature:-_____

Date:	Time
Purpose:-	
Location - Origin	Destination
Odometer start	Odometer Finish
Gas fill up :- Yes/No	If yes Gallons filled
Cost per gallon	Amount paid
Paid Parking:-	Paid Tolls:-

Date:	Time
Purpose:-	
Location - Origin	Destination
Odometer start	Odometer Finish
Gas fill up :- Yes/No	If yes Gallons filled
Cost per gallon	Amount paid
Paid Parking:-	Paid Tolls:-

Mileage Log Book

Employee ID :- _____ Name:- _____

Title :-_____ Dept:- _____

Vehicle Id _____ Signature:-_____

Date: Time

Purpose:-

Location - Origin	Destination
Odometer start	Odometer Finish
Gas fill up :- Yes/No	If yes Gallons filled
Cost per gallon	Amount paid
Paid Parking:-	Paid Tolls:-

Date: Time

Purpose:-

Location - Origin	Destination
Odometer start	Odometer Finish
Gas fill up :- Yes/No	If yes Gallons filled
Cost per gallon	Amount paid
Paid Parking:-	Paid Tolls:-

Mileage Log Book

Employee ID :- _____ Name:- _____

Title :-_____ Dept:- _____

Vehicle Id _____ Signature:-_____

Date:	Time
Purpose:-	
Location - Origin	Destination
Odometer start	Odometer Finish
Gas fill up :- Yes/No	If yes Gallons filled
Cost per gallon	Amount paid
Paid Parking:-	Paid Tolls:-

Date:	Time
Purpose:-	
Location - Origin	Destination
Odometer start	Odometer Finish
Gas fill up :- Yes/No	If yes Gallons filled
Cost per gallon	Amount paid
Paid Parking:-	Paid Tolls:-

Mileage Log Book

Employee ID :- _____ Name:- _____

Title :-_____ Dept:- _____

Vehicle Id _____ Signature:-_____

Date:	Time
Purpose:-	
Location - Origin	Destination
Odometer start	Odometer Finish
Gas fill up :- Yes/No	If yes Gallons filled
Cost per gallon	Amount paid
Paid Parking:-	Paid Tolls:-

Date:	Time
Purpose:-	
Location - Origin	Destination
Odometer start	Odometer Finish
Gas fill up :- Yes/No	If yes Gallons filled
Cost per gallon	Amount paid
Paid Parking:-	Paid Tolls:-

Mileage Log Book

Employee ID :- _____ Name:- _____

Title :-_____ Dept:- _____

Vehicle Id _____ Signature:-_____

Date:	Time
Purpose:-	
Location - Origin	Destination
Odometer start	Odometer Finish
Gas fill up :- Yes/No	If yes Gallons filled
Cost per gallon	Amount paid
Paid Parking:-	Paid Tolls:-

Date:	Time
Purpose:-	
Location - Origin	Destination
Odometer start	Odometer Finish
Gas fill up :- Yes/No	If yes Gallons filled
Cost per gallon	Amount paid
Paid Parking:-	Paid Tolls:-

Mileage Log Book

Employee ID :- _____ Name:- _____

Title :-_____ Dept:- _____

Vehicle Id _____ Signature:-_____

Date:	Time
Purpose:-	
Location - Origin	Destination
Odometer start	Odometer Finish
Gas fill up :- Yes/No	If yes Gallons filled
Cost per gallon	Amount paid
Paid Parking:-	Paid Tolls:-

Date:	Time
Purpose:-	
Location - Origin	Destination
Odometer start	Odometer Finish
Gas fill up :- Yes/No	If yes Gallons filled
Cost per gallon	Amount paid
Paid Parking:-	Paid Tolls:-

Mileage Log Book

Employee ID :- _____ Name:- _____

Title :-_____ Dept:- _____

Vehicle Id _____ Signature:-_____

Date:	Time
Purpose:-	
Location - Origin	Destination
Odometer start	Odometer Finish
Gas fill up :- Yes/No	If yes Gallons filled
Cost per gallon	Amount paid
Paid Parking:-	Paid Tolls:-
Date:	Time
Purpose:-	
Location - Origin	Destination
Odometer start	Odometer Finish
Gas fill up :- Yes/No	If yes Gallons filled
Cost per gallon	Amount paid
Paid Parking:-	Paid Tolls:-

Mileage Log Book

Employee ID :- _____ Name:- _____

Title :-_____ Dept:- _____

Vehicle Id _____ Signature:-_____

Date:	Time
Purpose:-	
Location - Origin	Destination
Odometer start	Odometer Finish
Gas fill up :- Yes/No	If yes Gallons filled
Cost per gallon	Amount paid
Paid Parking:-	Paid Tolls:-

- -

Date:	Time
Purpose:-	
Location - Origin	Destination
Odometer start	Odometer Finish
Gas fill up :- Yes/No	If yes Gallons filled
Cost per gallon	Amount paid
Paid Parking:-	Paid Tolls:-

Mileage Log Book

Employee ID :- _____ Name:- _____

Title :-_____ Dept:- _____

Vehicle Id _____ Signature:-_____

Date:	Time
Purpose:-	
Location - Origin	Destination
Odometer start	Odometer Finish
Gas fill up :- Yes/No	If yes Gallons filled
Cost per gallon	Amount paid
Paid Parking:-	Paid Tolls:-

Date:	Time
Purpose:-	
Location - Origin	Destination
Odometer start	Odometer Finish
Gas fill up :- Yes/No	If yes Gallons filled
Cost per gallon	Amount paid
Paid Parking:-	Paid Tolls:-

Mileage Log Book

Employee ID :- _____ Name:- _____

Title :-_____ Dept:- _____

Vehicle Id _____ Signature:-_____

Date:	Time

Purpose:-

Location - Origin	Destination
Odometer start	Odometer Finish
Gas fill up :- Yes/No	If yes Gallons filled
Cost per gallon	Amount paid
Paid Parking:-	Paid Tolls:-

Date:	Time

Purpose:-

Location - Origin	Destination
Odometer start	Odometer Finish
Gas fill up :- Yes/No	If yes Gallons filled
Cost per gallon	Amount paid
Paid Parking:-	Paid Tolls:-

Mileage Log Book

Employee ID :- _____ Name:- _____

Title :-_____ Dept:- _____

Vehicle Id _____ Signature:-_____

Date: Time

Purpose:-

Location - Origin   Destination

Odometer start   Odometer Finish

Gas fill up :- Yes/No   If yes Gallons filled

Cost per gallon   Amount paid

Paid Parking:-   Paid Tolls:-

Date: Time

Purpose:-

Location - Origin   Destination

Odometer start   Odometer Finish

Gas fill up :- Yes/No   If yes Gallons filled

Cost per gallon   Amount paid

Paid Parking:-   Paid Tolls:-

Mileage Log Book

Employee ID :- _____ Name:- _____

Title :-_____ Dept:- _____

Vehicle Id _____ Signature:-_____

Date:	Time
Purpose:-	
Location - Origin	Destination
Odometer start	Odometer Finish
Gas fill up :- Yes/No	If yes Gallons filled
Cost per gallon	Amount paid
Paid Parking:-	Paid Tolls:-

Date:	Time
Purpose:-	
Location - Origin	Destination
Odometer start	Odometer Finish
Gas fill up :- Yes/No	If yes Gallons filled
Cost per gallon	Amount paid
Paid Parking:-	Paid Tolls:-

Mileage Log Book

Employee ID :- _____ Name:- _____

Title :-_____ Dept:- _____

Vehicle Id _____ Signature:-_____

Date: | Time

Purpose:-

Location - Origin | Destination

Odometer start | Odometer Finish

Gas fill up :- Yes/No | If yes Gallons filled

Cost per gallon | Amount paid

Paid Parking:- | Paid Tolls:-

Date: | Time

Purpose:-

Location - Origin | Destination

Odometer start | Odometer Finish

Gas fill up :- Yes/No | If yes Gallons filled

Cost per gallon | Amount paid

Paid Parking:- | Paid Tolls:-

Mileage Log Book

Employee ID :- _____ Name:- _____

Title :-_____ Dept:- _____

Vehicle Id _____ Signature:-_____

Date: _____ Time _____

Purpose:-

Location - Origin	Destination
Odometer start	Odometer Finish
Gas fill up :- Yes/No	If yes Gallons filled
Cost per gallon	Amount paid
Paid Parking:-	Paid Tolls:-

Date: _____ Time _____

Purpose:-

Location - Origin	Destination
Odometer start	Odometer Finish
Gas fill up :- Yes/No	If yes Gallons filled
Cost per gallon	Amount paid
Paid Parking:-	Paid Tolls:-

Mileage Log Book

Employee ID :- _____ Name:- _____

Title :-_____ Dept:- _____

Vehicle Id _____ Signature:-_____

Date:	Time
Purpose:-	
Location - Origin	Destination
Odometer start	Odometer Finish
Gas fill up :- Yes/No	If yes Gallons filled
Cost per gallon	Amount paid
Paid Parking:-	Paid Tolls:-

Date:	Time
Purpose:-	
Location - Origin	Destination
Odometer start	Odometer Finish
Gas fill up :- Yes/No	If yes Gallons filled
Cost per gallon	Amount paid
Paid Parking:-	Paid Tolls:-

Mileage Log Book

Employee ID :- _____ Name:- _____

Title :-_____ Dept:- _____

Vehicle Id _____ Signature:-_____

Date: | Time

Purpose:-

Location - Origin | Destination

Odometer start | Odometer Finish

Gas fill up :- Yes/No | If yes Gallons filled

Cost per gallon | Amount paid

Paid Parking:- | Paid Tolls:-

Date: | Time

Purpose:-

Location - Origin | Destination

Odometer start | Odometer Finish

Gas fill up :- Yes/No | If yes Gallons filled

Cost per gallon | Amount paid

Paid Parking:- | Paid Tolls:-

Mileage Log Book

Employee ID :- _____ Name:- _____

Title :-_____ Dept:- _____

Vehicle Id _____ Signature:-_____

Date:	Time
Purpose:-	
Location - Origin	Destination
Odometer start	Odometer Finish
Gas fill up :- Yes/No	If yes Gallons filled
Cost per gallon	Amount paid
Paid Parking:-	Paid Tolls:-

Date:	Time
Purpose:-	
Location - Origin	Destination
Odometer start	Odometer Finish
Gas fill up :- Yes/No	If yes Gallons filled
Cost per gallon	Amount paid
Paid Parking:-	Paid Tolls:-

Mileage Log Book

Employee ID :- _____ Name:- _____

Title :-_____ Dept:- _____

Vehicle Id _____ Signature:-_____

Date: Time

Purpose:-

Location - Origin	Destination
Odometer start	Odometer Finish
Gas fill up :- Yes/No	If yes Gallons filled
Cost per gallon	Amount paid
Paid Parking:-	Paid Tolls:-

Date: Time

Purpose:-

Location - Origin	Destination
Odometer start	Odometer Finish
Gas fill up :- Yes/No	If yes Gallons filled
Cost per gallon	Amount paid
Paid Parking:-	Paid Tolls:-

Mileage Log Book

Employee ID :- _____ Name:- _____

Title :-_____ Dept:- _____

Vehicle Id _____ Signature:-_____

Date:	Time
Purpose:-	
Location - Origin	Destination
Odometer start	Odometer Finish
Gas fill up :- Yes/No	If yes Gallons filled
Cost per gallon	Amount paid
Paid Parking:-	Paid Tolls:-
Date:	Time
Purpose:-	
Location - Origin	Destination
Odometer start	Odometer Finish
Gas fill up :- Yes/No	If yes Gallons filled
Cost per gallon	Amount paid
Paid Parking:-	Paid Tolls:-

Mileage Log Book

Employee ID :- _____ Name:- _____

Title :-_____ Dept:- _____

Vehicle Id _____ Signature:-_____

Date: _____ Time _____

Purpose:- _____

Location - Origin	Destination
Odometer start	Odometer Finish
Gas fill up :- Yes/No	If yes Gallons filled
Cost per gallon	Amount paid
Paid Parking:-	Paid Tolls:-

Date: _____ Time _____

Purpose:- _____

Location - Origin	Destination
Odometer start	Odometer Finish
Gas fill up :- Yes/No	If yes Gallons filled
Cost per gallon	Amount paid
Paid Parking:-	Paid Tolls:-

Mileage Log Book

Employee ID :- _____ Name:- _____

Title :-_____ Dept:- _____

Vehicle Id _____ Signature:-_____

Date: Time

Purpose:-

Location - Origin	Destination
Odometer start	Odometer Finish
Gas fill up :- Yes/No	If yes Gallons filled
Cost per gallon	Amount paid
Paid Parking:-	Paid Tolls:-

Date: Time

Purpose:-

Location - Origin	Destination
Odometer start	Odometer Finish
Gas fill up :- Yes/No	If yes Gallons filled
Cost per gallon	Amount paid
Paid Parking:-	Paid Tolls:-

Mileage Log Book

Employee ID :- _____ Name:- _____

Title :-_____ Dept:- _____

Vehicle Id _____ Signature:-_____

Date: | Time

Purpose:-

Location - Origin | Destination

Odometer start | Odometer Finish

Gas fill up :- Yes/No | If yes Gallons filled

Cost per gallon | Amount paid

Paid Parking:- | Paid Tolls:-

- -

Date: | Time

Purpose:-

Location - Origin | Destination

Odometer start | Odometer Finish

Gas fill up :- Yes/No | If yes Gallons filled

Cost per gallon | Amount paid

Paid Parking:- | Paid Tolls:-

Mileage Log Book

Employee ID :- _____ Name:- _____

Title :-_____ Dept:- _____

Vehicle Id _____ Signature:-_____

Date:	Time
Purpose:-	
Location - Origin	Destination
Odometer start	Odometer Finish
Gas fill up :- Yes/No	If yes Gallons filled
Cost per gallon	Amount paid
Paid Parking:-	Paid Tolls:-

Date:	Time
Purpose:-	
Location - Origin	Destination
Odometer start	Odometer Finish
Gas fill up :- Yes/No	If yes Gallons filled
Cost per gallon	Amount paid
Paid Parking:-	Paid Tolls:-

Mileage Log Book

Employee ID :- _____ Name:- _____

Title :-_____ Dept:- _____

Vehicle Id _____ Signature:-_____

Date:	Time
Purpose:-	
Location - Origin	Destination
Odometer start	Odometer Finish
Gas fill up :- Yes/No	If yes Gallons filled
Cost per gallon	Amount paid
Paid Parking:-	Paid Tolls:-

Date:	Time
Purpose:-	
Location - Origin	Destination
Odometer start	Odometer Finish
Gas fill up :- Yes/No	If yes Gallons filled
Cost per gallon	Amount paid
Paid Parking:-	Paid Tolls:-

Mileage Log Book

Employee ID :- _____ Name:- _____

Title :-_____ Dept:- _____

Vehicle Id _____ Signature:- _____

Date: Time

Purpose:-

Location - Origin	Destination
Odometer start	Odometer Finish
Gas fill up :- Yes/No	If yes Gallons filled
Cost per gallon	Amount paid
Paid Parking:-	Paid Tolls:-

Date: Time

Purpose:-

Location - Origin	Destination
Odometer start	Odometer Finish
Gas fill up :- Yes/No	If yes Gallons filled
Cost per gallon	Amount paid
Paid Parking:-	Paid Tolls:-

Mileage Log Book

Employee ID :- _____ Name:- _____

Title :-_____ Dept:- _____

Vehicle Id _____ Signature:-_____

Date:	Time
Purpose:-	
Location - Origin	Destination
Odometer start	Odometer Finish
Gas fill up :- Yes/No	If yes Gallons filled
Cost per gallon	Amount paid
Paid Parking:-	Paid Tolls:-

Date:	Time
Purpose:-	
Location - Origin	Destination
Odometer start	Odometer Finish
Gas fill up :- Yes/No	If yes Gallons filled
Cost per gallon	Amount paid
Paid Parking:-	Paid Tolls:-

Mileage Log Book

Employee ID :- _____ Name:- _____

Title :-_____ Dept:- _____

Vehicle Id _____ Signature:-_____

Date:	Time
Purpose:-	
Location - Origin	Destination
Odometer start	Odometer Finish
Gas fill up :- Yes/No	If yes Gallons filled
Cost per gallon	Amount paid
Paid Parking:-	Paid Tolls:-

Date:	Time
Purpose:-	
Location - Origin	Destination
Odometer start	Odometer Finish
Gas fill up :- Yes/No	If yes Gallons filled
Cost per gallon	Amount paid
Paid Parking:-	Paid Tolls:-

Mileage Log Book

Employee ID :- _____ Name:- _____

Title :-_____ Dept:- _____

Vehicle Id _____ Signature:-_____

Date: _____ Time _____

Purpose:-

Location - Origin	Destination
Odometer start	Odometer Finish
Gas fill up :- Yes/No	If yes Gallons filled
Cost per gallon	Amount paid
Paid Parking:-	Paid Tolls:-

Date: _____ Time _____

Purpose:-

Location - Origin	Destination
Odometer start	Odometer Finish
Gas fill up :- Yes/No	If yes Gallons filled
Cost per gallon	Amount paid
Paid Parking:-	Paid Tolls:-

Mileage Log Book

Employee ID :- _____ Name:- _____

Title :-_____ Dept:- _____

Vehicle Id _____ Signature:-_____

Date: Time

Purpose:-

Location - Origin	Destination
Odometer start	Odometer Finish
Gas fill up :- Yes/No	If yes Gallons filled
Cost per gallon	Amount paid
Paid Parking:-	Paid Tolls:-

Date: Time

Purpose:-

Location - Origin	Destination
Odometer start	Odometer Finish
Gas fill up :- Yes/No	If yes Gallons filled
Cost per gallon	Amount paid
Paid Parking:-	Paid Tolls:-

Mileage Log Book

Employee ID :- _____ Name:- _____

Title :-_____ Dept:- _____

Vehicle Id _____ Signature:-_____

Date: Time

Purpose:-

Location - Origin   Destination

Odometer start   Odometer Finish

Gas fill up :- Yes/No   If yes Gallons filled

Cost per gallon   Amount paid

Paid Parking:-   Paid Tolls:-

Date: Time

Purpose:-

Location - Origin   Destination

Odometer start   Odometer Finish

Gas fill up :- Yes/No   If yes Gallons filled

Cost per gallon   Amount paid

Paid Parking:-   Paid Tolls:-

Mileage Log Book

Employee ID :- _____ Name:- _____

Title :-_____ Dept:- _____

Vehicle Id _____ Signature:-_____

Date: Time

Purpose:-

Location - Origin	Destination
Odometer start	Odometer Finish
Gas fill up :- Yes/No	If yes Gallons filled
Cost per gallon	Amount paid
Paid Parking:-	Paid Tolls:-

Date: Time

Purpose:-

Location - Origin	Destination
Odometer start	Odometer Finish
Gas fill up :- Yes/No	If yes Gallons filled
Cost per gallon	Amount paid
Paid Parking:-	Paid Tolls:-

Mileage Log Book

Employee ID :- _____ Name:- _____

Title :-_____ Dept:- _____

Vehicle Id _____ Signature:-_____

Date: Time

Purpose:-

Location - Origin	Destination
Odometer start	Odometer Finish
Gas fill up :- Yes/No	If yes Gallons filled
Cost per gallon	Amount paid
Paid Parking:-	Paid Tolls:-

Date: Time

Purpose:-

Location - Origin	Destination
Odometer start	Odometer Finish
Gas fill up :- Yes/No	If yes Gallons filled
Cost per gallon	Amount paid
Paid Parking:-	Paid Tolls:-

Mileage Log Book

Employee ID :- _____ Name:- _____

Title :-_____ Dept:- _____

Vehicle Id _____ Signature:-_____

Date: Time

Purpose:-

Location - Origin	Destination
Odometer start	Odometer Finish
Gas fill up :- Yes/No	If yes Gallons filled
Cost per gallon	Amount paid
Paid Parking:-	Paid Tolls:-

Date: Time

Purpose:-

Location - Origin	Destination
Odometer start	Odometer Finish
Gas fill up :- Yes/No	If yes Gallons filled
Cost per gallon	Amount paid
Paid Parking:-	Paid Tolls:-

Mileage Log Book

Employee ID :- _____ Name:- _____

Title :-_____ Dept:- _____

Vehicle Id _____ Signature:-_____

Date:	Time
Purpose:-	
Location - Origin	Destination
Odometer start	Odometer Finish
Gas fill up :- Yes/No	If yes Gallons filled
Cost per gallon	Amount paid
Paid Parking:-	Paid Tolls:-

Date:	Time
Purpose:-	
Location - Origin	Destination
Odometer start	Odometer Finish
Gas fill up :- Yes/No	If yes Gallons filled
Cost per gallon	Amount paid
Paid Parking:-	Paid Tolls:-

Mileage Log Book

Employee ID :- _____ Name:- _____

Title :- _____ Dept:- _____

Vehicle Id _____ Signature:- _____

Date: Time

Purpose:-

Location - Origin   Destination

Odometer start   Odometer Finish

Gas fill up :- Yes/No   If yes Gallons filled

Cost per gallon   Amount paid

Paid Parking:-   Paid Tolls:-

Date: Time

Purpose:-

Location - Origin   Destination

Odometer start   Odometer Finish

Gas fill up :- Yes/No   If yes Gallons filled

Cost per gallon   Amount paid

Paid Parking:-   Paid Tolls:-

Mileage Log Book

Employee ID :- _____ Name:- _____

Title :-_____ Dept:- _____

Vehicle Id _____ Signature:-_____

Date:	Time
Purpose:-	
Location - Origin	Destination
Odometer start	Odometer Finish
Gas fill up :- Yes/No	If yes Gallons filled
Cost per gallon	Amount paid
Paid Parking:-	Paid Tolls:-

Date:	Time
Purpose:-	
Location - Origin	Destination
Odometer start	Odometer Finish
Gas fill up :- Yes/No	If yes Gallons filled
Cost per gallon	Amount paid
Paid Parking:-	Paid Tolls:-

Mileage Log Book

Employee ID :- _____ Name:- _____

Title :-_____ Dept:- _____

Vehicle Id _____ Signature:-_____

Date:	Time
Purpose:-	
Location - Origin	Destination
Odometer start	Odometer Finish
Gas fill up :- Yes/No	If yes Gallons filled
Cost per gallon	Amount paid
Paid Parking:-	Paid Tolls:-

Date:	Time
Purpose:-	
Location - Origin	Destination
Odometer start	Odometer Finish
Gas fill up :- Yes/No	If yes Gallons filled
Cost per gallon	Amount paid
Paid Parking:-	Paid Tolls:-

Mileage Log Book

Employee ID :- _____ Name:- _____

Title :-_____ Dept:- _____

Vehicle Id _____ Signature:-_____

Date: Time

Purpose:-

Location - Origin	Destination
Odometer start	Odometer Finish
Gas fill up :- Yes/No	If yes Gallons filled
Cost per gallon	Amount paid
Paid Parking:-	Paid Tolls:-

Date: Time

Purpose:-

Location - Origin	Destination
Odometer start	Odometer Finish
Gas fill up :- Yes/No	If yes Gallons filled
Cost per gallon	Amount paid
Paid Parking:-	Paid Tolls:-

Mileage Log Book

Employee ID :- _____ Name:- _____

Title :-_____ Dept:- _____

Vehicle Id _____ Signature:-_____

Date:	Time
Purpose:-	
Location - Origin	Destination
Odometer start	Odometer Finish
Gas fill up :- Yes/No	If yes Gallons filled
Cost per gallon	Amount paid
Paid Parking:-	Paid Tolls:-

Date:	Time
Purpose:-	
Location - Origin	Destination
Odometer start	Odometer Finish
Gas fill up :- Yes/No	If yes Gallons filled
Cost per gallon	Amount paid
Paid Parking:-	Paid Tolls:-

Mileage Log Book

Employee ID :- _____ Name:- _____

Title :-_____ Dept:- _____

Vehicle Id _____ Signature:-_____

Date: _____ Time _____

Purpose:-

Location - Origin	Destination
Odometer start	Odometer Finish
Gas fill up :- Yes/No	If yes Gallons filled
Cost per gallon	Amount paid
Paid Parking:-	Paid Tolls:-

Date: _____ Time _____

Purpose:-

Location - Origin	Destination
Odometer start	Odometer Finish
Gas fill up :- Yes/No	If yes Gallons filled
Cost per gallon	Amount paid
Paid Parking:-	Paid Tolls:-

Mileage Log Book

Employee ID :- _____ Name:- _____

Title :-_____ Dept:- _____

Vehicle Id _____ Signature:-_____

Date:	Time
Purpose:-	
Location - Origin	Destination
Odometer start	Odometer Finish
Gas fill up :- Yes/No	If yes Gallons filled
Cost per gallon	Amount paid
Paid Parking:-	Paid Tolls:-

Date:	Time
Purpose:-	
Location - Origin	Destination
Odometer start	Odometer Finish
Gas fill up :- Yes/No	If yes Gallons filled
Cost per gallon	Amount paid
Paid Parking:-	Paid Tolls:-

Mileage Log Book

Employee ID :- _____ Name:- _____

Title :-_____ Dept:- _____

Vehicle Id _____ Signature:-_____

Date: Time

Purpose:-

Location - Origin	Destination
Odometer start	Odometer Finish
Gas fill up :- Yes/No	If yes Gallons filled
Cost per gallon	Amount paid
Paid Parking:-	Paid Tolls:-

Date: Time

Purpose:-

Location - Origin	Destination
Odometer start	Odometer Finish
Gas fill up :- Yes/No	If yes Gallons filled
Cost per gallon	Amount paid
Paid Parking:-	Paid Tolls:-

Mileage Log Book

Employee ID :- _____ Name:- _____

Title :-_____ Dept:- _____

Vehicle Id _____ Signature:-_____

Date: Time

Purpose:-

Location - Origin	Destination
Odometer start	Odometer Finish
Gas fill up :- Yes/No	If yes Gallons filled
Cost per gallon	Amount paid
Paid Parking:-	Paid Tolls:-

Date: Time

Purpose:-

Location - Origin	Destination
Odometer start	Odometer Finish
Gas fill up :- Yes/No	If yes Gallons filled
Cost per gallon	Amount paid
Paid Parking:-	Paid Tolls:-

Mileage Log Book

Employee ID :- _____ Name:- _____

Title :-_____ Dept:- _____

Vehicle Id _____ Signature:-_____

Date:	Time
Purpose:-	
Location - Origin	Destination
Odometer start	Odometer Finish
Gas fill up :- Yes/No	If yes Gallons filled
Cost per gallon	Amount paid
Paid Parking:-	Paid Tolls:-

Date:	Time
Purpose:-	
Location - Origin	Destination
Odometer start	Odometer Finish
Gas fill up :- Yes/No	If yes Gallons filled
Cost per gallon	Amount paid
Paid Parking:-	Paid Tolls:-

Mileage Log Book

Employee ID :- _____ Name:- _____

Title :-_____ Dept:- _____

Vehicle Id _____ Signature:-_____

Date:	Time
Purpose:-	
Location - Origin	Destination
Odometer start	Odometer Finish
Gas fill up :- Yes/No	If yes Gallons filled
Cost per gallon	Amount paid
Paid Parking:-	Paid Tolls:-
Date:	Time
Purpose:-	
Location - Origin	Destination
Odometer start	Odometer Finish
Gas fill up :- Yes/No	If yes Gallons filled
Cost per gallon	Amount paid
Paid Parking:-	Paid Tolls:-

Mileage Log Book

Employee ID :- _____ Name:- _____

Title :- _____ Dept:- _____

Vehicle Id _____ Signature:- _____

Date: | Time

Purpose:-

Location - Origin | Destination

Odometer start | Odometer Finish

Gas fill up :- Yes/No | If yes Gallons filled

Cost per gallon | Amount paid

Paid Parking:- | Paid Tolls:-

Date: | Time

Purpose:-

Location - Origin | Destination

Odometer start | Odometer Finish

Gas fill up :- Yes/No | If yes Gallons filled

Cost per gallon | Amount paid

Paid Parking:- | Paid Tolls:-

Mileage Log Book

Employee ID :- _____ Name:- _____

Title :-_____ Dept:- _____

Vehicle Id _____ Signature:-_____

Date: Time

Purpose:-

Location - Origin	Destination
Odometer start	Odometer Finish
Gas fill up :- Yes/No	If yes Gallons filled
Cost per gallon	Amount paid
Paid Parking:-	Paid Tolls:-

Date: Time

Purpose:-

Location - Origin	Destination
Odometer start	Odometer Finish
Gas fill up :- Yes/No	If yes Gallons filled
Cost per gallon	Amount paid
Paid Parking:-	Paid Tolls:-

Mileage Log Book

Employee ID :- _____ Name:- _____

Title :-_____ Dept:- _____

Vehicle Id _____ Signature:-_____

Date:	Time
Purpose:-	
Location - Origin	Destination
Odometer start	Odometer Finish
Gas fill up :- Yes/No	If yes Gallons filled
Cost per gallon	Amount paid
Paid Parking:-	Paid Tolls:-

Date:	Time
Purpose:-	
Location - Origin	Destination
Odometer start	Odometer Finish
Gas fill up :- Yes/No	If yes Gallons filled
Cost per gallon	Amount paid
Paid Parking:-	Paid Tolls:-

Mileage Log Book

Employee ID :- _____ Name:- _____

Title :-_____ Dept:- _____

Vehicle Id _____ Signature:-_____

Date: _____ Time _____

Purpose:- _____

Location - Origin _____ Destination _____

Odometer start _____ Odometer Finish _____

Gas fill up :- Yes/No _____ If yes Gallons filled _____

Cost per gallon _____ Amount paid _____

Paid Parking:- _____ Paid Tolls:- _____

Date: _____ Time _____

Purpose:- _____

Location - Origin _____ Destination _____

Odometer start _____ Odometer Finish _____

Gas fill up :- Yes/No _____ If yes Gallons filled _____

Cost per gallon _____ Amount paid _____

Paid Parking:- _____ Paid Tolls:- _____

Mileage Log Book

Employee ID :- _____ Name:- _____

Title :-_____ Dept:- _____

Vehicle Id _____ Signature:-_____

Date:	Time
Purpose:-	
Location - Origin	Destination
Odometer start	Odometer Finish
Gas fill up :- Yes/No	If yes Gallons filled
Cost per gallon	Amount paid
Paid Parking:-	Paid Tolls:-

Date:	Time
Purpose:-	
Location - Origin	Destination
Odometer start	Odometer Finish
Gas fill up :- Yes/No	If yes Gallons filled
Cost per gallon	Amount paid
Paid Parking:-	Paid Tolls:-

Mileage Log Book

Employee ID :- _____ Name:- _____

Title :-_____ Dept:- _____

Vehicle Id _____ Signature:-_____

Date: Time

Purpose:-

Location - Origin	Destination
Odometer start	Odometer Finish
Gas fill up :- Yes/No	If yes Gallons filled
Cost per gallon	Amount paid
Paid Parking:-	Paid Tolls:-

Date: Time

Purpose:-

Location - Origin	Destination
Odometer start	Odometer Finish
Gas fill up :- Yes/No	If yes Gallons filled
Cost per gallon	Amount paid
Paid Parking:-	Paid Tolls:-

Mileage Log Book

Employee ID :- _____ Name:- _____

Title :-_____ Dept:- _____

Vehicle Id _____ Signature:-_____

Date: | Time

Purpose:-

Location - Origin | Destination

Odometer start | Odometer Finish

Gas fill up :- Yes/No | If yes Gallons filled

Cost per gallon | Amount paid

Paid Parking:- | Paid Tolls:-

Date: | Time

Purpose:-

Location - Origin | Destination

Odometer start | Odometer Finish

Gas fill up :- Yes/No | If yes Gallons filled

Cost per gallon | Amount paid

Paid Parking:- | Paid Tolls:-

Mileage Log Book

Employee ID :- _____ Name:- _____

Title :-_____ Dept:- _____

Vehicle Id _____ Signature:-_____

Date: Time

Purpose:-

Location - Origin   Destination

Odometer start   Odometer Finish

Gas fill up :- Yes/No   If yes Gallons filled

Cost per gallon   Amount paid

Paid Parking:-   Paid Tolls:-

Date: Time

Purpose:-

Location - Origin   Destination

Odometer start   Odometer Finish

Gas fill up :- Yes/No   If yes Gallons filled

Cost per gallon   Amount paid

Paid Parking:-   Paid Tolls:-

Mileage Log Book

Employee ID :- _____ Name:- _____

Title :-_____ Dept:- _____

Vehicle Id _____ Signature:-_____

Date:	Time
Purpose:-	
Location - Origin	Destination
Odometer start	Odometer Finish
Gas fill up :- Yes/No	If yes Gallons filled
Cost per gallon	Amount paid
Paid Parking:-	Paid Tolls:-

- -

Date:	Time
Purpose:-	
Location - Origin	Destination
Odometer start	Odometer Finish
Gas fill up :- Yes/No	If yes Gallons filled
Cost per gallon	Amount paid
Paid Parking:-	Paid Tolls:-

Mileage Log Book

Employee ID :- _____ Name:- _____

Title :-_____ Dept:- _____

Vehicle Id _____ Signature:-_____

Date: Time

Purpose:-

Location - Origin	Destination
Odometer start	Odometer Finish
Gas fill up :- Yes/No	If yes Gallons filled
Cost per gallon	Amount paid
Paid Parking:-	Paid Tolls:-

Date: Time

Purpose:-

Location - Origin	Destination
Odometer start	Odometer Finish
Gas fill up :- Yes/No	If yes Gallons filled
Cost per gallon	Amount paid
Paid Parking:-	Paid Tolls:-

Mileage Log Book

Employee ID :- _____ Name:- _____

Title :-_____ Dept:- _____

Vehicle Id _____ Signature:-_____

Date:	Time
Purpose:-	
Location - Origin	Destination
Odometer start	Odometer Finish
Gas fill up :- Yes/No	If yes Gallons filled
Cost per gallon	Amount paid
Paid Parking:-	Paid Tolls:-

Date:	Time
Purpose:-	
Location - Origin	Destination
Odometer start	Odometer Finish
Gas fill up :- Yes/No	If yes Gallons filled
Cost per gallon	Amount paid
Paid Parking:-	Paid Tolls:-

Mileage Log Book

Employee ID :- _____ Name:- _____

Title :-_____ Dept:- _____

Vehicle Id _____ Signature:-_____

Date:	Time
Purpose:-	
Location - Origin	Destination
Odometer start	Odometer Finish
Gas fill up :- Yes/No	If yes Gallons filled
Cost per gallon	Amount paid
Paid Parking:-	Paid Tolls:-
Date:	Time
Purpose:-	
Location - Origin	Destination
Odometer start	Odometer Finish
Gas fill up :- Yes/No	If yes Gallons filled
Cost per gallon	Amount paid
Paid Parking:-	Paid Tolls:-

Mileage Log Book

Employee ID :- _____ Name:- _____

Title :-_____ Dept:- _____

Vehicle Id _____ Signature:-_____

Date: Time

Purpose:-

Location - Origin	Destination
Odometer start	Odometer Finish
Gas fill up :- Yes/No	If yes Gallons filled
Cost per gallon	Amount paid
Paid Parking:-	Paid Tolls:-

Date: Time

Purpose:-

Location - Origin	Destination
Odometer start	Odometer Finish
Gas fill up :- Yes/No	If yes Gallons filled
Cost per gallon	Amount paid
Paid Parking:-	Paid Tolls:-

Mileage Log Book

Employee ID :- _____ Name:- _____

Title :-_____ Dept:- _____

Vehicle Id _____ Signature:-_____

Date: Time

Purpose:-

Location - Origin	Destination
Odometer start	Odometer Finish
Gas fill up :- Yes/No	If yes Gallons filled
Cost per gallon	Amount paid
Paid Parking:-	Paid Tolls:-

Date: Time

Purpose:-

Location - Origin	Destination
Odometer start	Odometer Finish
Gas fill up :- Yes/No	If yes Gallons filled
Cost per gallon	Amount paid
Paid Parking:-	Paid Tolls:-

Mileage Log Book

Employee ID :- _____ Name:- _____

Title :-_____ Dept:- _____

Vehicle Id _____ Signature:-_____

Date: _____ Time _____

Purpose:- _____

Location - Origin	Destination
Odometer start	Odometer Finish
Gas fill up :- Yes/No	If yes Gallons filled
Cost per gallon	Amount paid
Paid Parking:-	Paid Tolls:-

Date: _____ Time _____

Purpose:- _____

Location - Origin	Destination
Odometer start	Odometer Finish
Gas fill up :- Yes/No	If yes Gallons filled
Cost per gallon	Amount paid
Paid Parking:-	Paid Tolls:-

Mileage Log Book

Employee ID :- _____ Name:- _____

Title :-_____ Dept:- _____

Vehicle Id _____ Signature:-_____

Date:	Time
Purpose:-	
Location - Origin	Destination
Odometer start	Odometer Finish
Gas fill up :- Yes/No	If yes Gallons filled
Cost per gallon	Amount paid
Paid Parking:-	Paid Tolls:-

Date:	Time
Purpose:-	
Location - Origin	Destination
Odometer start	Odometer Finish
Gas fill up :- Yes/No	If yes Gallons filled
Cost per gallon	Amount paid
Paid Parking:-	Paid Tolls:-

Mileage Log Book

Employee ID :- _____ Name:- _____

Title :-_____ Dept:- _____

Vehicle Id _____ Signature:-_____

Date:	Time
Purpose:-	
Location - Origin	Destination
Odometer start	Odometer Finish
Gas fill up :- Yes/No	If yes Gallons filled
Cost per gallon	Amount paid
Paid Parking:-	Paid Tolls:-
Date:	Time
Purpose:-	
Location - Origin	Destination
Odometer start	Odometer Finish
Gas fill up :- Yes/No	If yes Gallons filled
Cost per gallon	Amount paid
Paid Parking:-	Paid Tolls:-

Mileage Log Book

Employee ID :- _____   Name:- _____

Title :-_____   Dept:- _____

Vehicle Id _____   Signature:-_____

Date:	Time
Purpose:-	
Location - Origin	Destination
Odometer start	Odometer Finish
Gas fill up :- Yes/No	If yes Gallons filled
Cost per gallon	Amount paid
Paid Parking:-	Paid Tolls:-

Date:	Time
Purpose:-	
Location - Origin	Destination
Odometer start	Odometer Finish
Gas fill up :- Yes/No	If yes Gallons filled
Cost per gallon	Amount paid
Paid Parking:-	Paid Tolls:-

Mileage Log Book

Employee ID :- _____ Name:- _____

Title :-_____ Dept:- _____

Vehicle Id _____ Signature:-_____

Date: | Time

Purpose:-

Location - Origin | Destination

Odometer start | Odometer Finish

Gas fill up :- Yes/No | If yes Gallons filled

Cost per gallon | Amount paid

Paid Parking:- | Paid Tolls:-

Date: | Time

Purpose:-

Location - Origin | Destination

Odometer start | Odometer Finish

Gas fill up :- Yes/No | If yes Gallons filled

Cost per gallon | Amount paid

Paid Parking:- | Paid Tolls:-

Mileage Log Book

Employee ID :- _____ Name:- _____

Title :-_____ Dept:- _____

Vehicle Id _____ Signature:-_____

Date: Time

Purpose:-

Location - Origin	Destination
Odometer start	Odometer Finish
Gas fill up :- Yes/No	If yes Gallons filled
Cost per gallon	Amount paid
Paid Parking:-	Paid Tolls:-

Date: Time

Purpose:-

Location - Origin	Destination
Odometer start	Odometer Finish
Gas fill up :- Yes/No	If yes Gallons filled
Cost per gallon	Amount paid
Paid Parking:-	Paid Tolls:-

Mileage Log Book

Employee ID :- _____ Name:- _____

Title :-_____ Dept:- _____

Vehicle Id _____ Signature:-_____

Date:	Time
Purpose:-	
Location - Origin	Destination
Odometer start	Odometer Finish
Gas fill up :- Yes/No	If yes Gallons filled
Cost per gallon	Amount paid
Paid Parking:-	Paid Tolls:-

- -

Date:	Time
Purpose:-	
Location - Origin	Destination
Odometer start	Odometer Finish
Gas fill up :- Yes/No	If yes Gallons filled
Cost per gallon	Amount paid
Paid Parking:-	Paid Tolls:-

Mileage Log Book

Employee ID :- _____ Name:- _____

Title :-_____ Dept:- _____

Vehicle Id _____ Signature:-_____

Date: Time

Purpose:-

Location - Origin	Destination
Odometer start	Odometer Finish
Gas fill up :- Yes/No	If yes Gallons filled
Cost per gallon	Amount paid
Paid Parking:-	Paid Tolls:-

Date: Time

Purpose:-

Location - Origin	Destination
Odometer start	Odometer Finish
Gas fill up :- Yes/No	If yes Gallons filled
Cost per gallon	Amount paid
Paid Parking:-	Paid Tolls:-

Mileage Log Book

Employee ID :- _____ Name:- _____

Title :-_____ Dept:- _____

Vehicle Id _____ Signature:-_____

Date: Time

Purpose:-

Location - Origin	Destination
Odometer start	Odometer Finish
Gas fill up :- Yes/No	If yes Gallons filled
Cost per gallon	Amount paid
Paid Parking:-	Paid Tolls:-

Date: Time

Purpose:-

Location - Origin	Destination
Odometer start	Odometer Finish
Gas fill up :- Yes/No	If yes Gallons filled
Cost per gallon	Amount paid
Paid Parking:-	Paid Tolls:-

Mileage Log Book

Employee ID :- _____ Name:- _____

Title :-_____ Dept:- _____

Vehicle Id _____ Signature:-_____

Date: Time

Purpose:-

Location - Origin	Destination
Odometer start	Odometer Finish
Gas fill up :- Yes/No	If yes Gallons filled
Cost per gallon	Amount paid
Paid Parking:-	Paid Tolls:-

Date: Time

Purpose:-

Location - Origin	Destination
Odometer start	Odometer Finish
Gas fill up :- Yes/No	If yes Gallons filled
Cost per gallon	Amount paid
Paid Parking:-	Paid Tolls:-

Mileage Log Book

Employee ID :- _____ Name:- _____

Title :-_____ Dept:- _____

Vehicle Id _____ Signature:-_____

Date:	Time
Purpose:-	
Location - Origin	Destination
Odometer start	Odometer Finish
Gas fill up :- Yes/No	If yes Gallons filled
Cost per gallon	Amount paid
Paid Parking:-	Paid Tolls:-
Date:	Time
Purpose:-	
Location - Origin	Destination
Odometer start	Odometer Finish
Gas fill up :- Yes/No	If yes Gallons filled
Cost per gallon	Amount paid
Paid Parking:-	Paid Tolls:-

Mileage Log Book

Employee ID :- _____ Name:- _____

Title :-_____ Dept:- _____

Vehicle Id _____ Signature:-_____

Date:	Time
Purpose:-	
Location - Origin	Destination
Odometer start	Odometer Finish
Gas fill up :- Yes/No	If yes Gallons filled
Cost per gallon	Amount paid
Paid Parking:-	Paid Tolls:-

Date:	Time
Purpose:-	
Location - Origin	Destination
Odometer start	Odometer Finish
Gas fill up :- Yes/No	If yes Gallons filled
Cost per gallon	Amount paid
Paid Parking:-	Paid Tolls:-

Mileage Log Book

Employee ID :- _____ Name:- _____

Title :-_____ Dept:- _____

Vehicle Id _____ Signature:-_____

Date:	Time
Purpose:-	
Location - Origin	Destination
Odometer start	Odometer Finish
Gas fill up :- Yes/No	If yes Gallons filled
Cost per gallon	Amount paid
Paid Parking:-	Paid Tolls:-

Date:	Time
Purpose:-	
Location - Origin	Destination
Odometer start	Odometer Finish
Gas fill up :- Yes/No	If yes Gallons filled
Cost per gallon	Amount paid
Paid Parking:-	Paid Tolls:-

Mileage Log Book

Employee ID :- _____ Name:- _____

Title :-_____ Dept:- _____

Vehicle Id _____ Signature:-_____

Date:	Time
Purpose:-	
Location - Origin	Destination
Odometer start	Odometer Finish
Gas fill up :- Yes/No	If yes Gallons filled
Cost per gallon	Amount paid
Paid Parking:-	Paid Tolls:-

Date:	Time
Purpose:-	
Location - Origin	Destination
Odometer start	Odometer Finish
Gas fill up :- Yes/No	If yes Gallons filled
Cost per gallon	Amount paid
Paid Parking:-	Paid Tolls:-

Mileage Log Book

Employee ID :- _____ Name:- _____

Title :-_____ Dept:- _____

Vehicle Id _____ Signature:-_____

Date:	Time
Purpose:-	
Location - Origin	Destination
Odometer start	Odometer Finish
Gas fill up :- Yes/No	If yes Gallons filled
Cost per gallon	Amount paid
Paid Parking:-	Paid Tolls:-

Date:	Time
Purpose:-	
Location - Origin	Destination
Odometer start	Odometer Finish
Gas fill up :- Yes/No	If yes Gallons filled
Cost per gallon	Amount paid
Paid Parking:-	Paid Tolls:-

Mileage Log Book

Employee ID :- _____ Name:- _____

Title :- _____ Dept:- _____

Vehicle Id _____ Signature:- _____

Date: | Time

Purpose:-

Location - Origin	Destination
Odometer start	Odometer Finish
Gas fill up :- Yes/No	If yes Gallons filled
Cost per gallon	Amount paid
Paid Parking:-	Paid Tolls:-

Date: | Time

Purpose:-

Location - Origin	Destination
Odometer start	Odometer Finish
Gas fill up :- Yes/No	If yes Gallons filled
Cost per gallon	Amount paid
Paid Parking:-	Paid Tolls:-

Mileage Log Book

Employee ID :- _____ Name:- _____

Title :-_____ Dept:- _____

Vehicle Id _____ Signature:-_____

Date: _____ Time _____

Purpose:- _____

Location - Origin	Destination
Odometer start	Odometer Finish
Gas fill up :- Yes/No	If yes Gallons filled
Cost per gallon	Amount paid
Paid Parking:-	Paid Tolls:-

Date: _____ Time _____

Purpose:- _____

Location - Origin	Destination
Odometer start	Odometer Finish
Gas fill up :- Yes/No	If yes Gallons filled
Cost per gallon	Amount paid
Paid Parking:-	Paid Tolls:-

Mileage Log Book

Employee ID :- _____ Name:- _____

Title :-_____ Dept:- _____

Vehicle Id _____ Signature:-_____

Date:	Time
Purpose:-	
Location - Origin	Destination
Odometer start	Odometer Finish
Gas fill up :- Yes/No	If yes Gallons filled
Cost per gallon	Amount paid
Paid Parking:-	Paid Tolls:-

Date:	Time
Purpose:-	
Location - Origin	Destination
Odometer start	Odometer Finish
Gas fill up :- Yes/No	If yes Gallons filled
Cost per gallon	Amount paid
Paid Parking:-	Paid Tolls:-

Mileage Log Book

Employee ID :- _____ Name:- _____

Title :-_____ Dept:- _____

Vehicle Id _____ Signature:-_____

Date: Time

Purpose:-

Location - Origin	Destination
Odometer start	Odometer Finish
Gas fill up :- Yes/No	If yes Gallons filled
Cost per gallon	Amount paid
Paid Parking:-	Paid Tolls:-

Date: Time

Purpose:-

Location - Origin	Destination
Odometer start	Odometer Finish
Gas fill up :- Yes/No	If yes Gallons filled
Cost per gallon	Amount paid
Paid Parking:-	Paid Tolls:-

Mileage Log Book

Employee ID :- _____ Name:- _____

Title :-_____ Dept:- _____

Vehicle Id _____ Signature:-_____

Date: Time

Purpose:-

Location - Origin   Destination

Odometer start   Odometer Finish

Gas fill up :- Yes/No   If yes Gallons filled

Cost per gallon   Amount paid

Paid Parking:-   Paid Tolls:-

- -

Date: Time

Purpose:-

Location - Origin   Destination

Odometer start   Odometer Finish

Gas fill up :- Yes/No   If yes Gallons filled

Cost per gallon   Amount paid

Paid Parking:-   Paid Tolls:-

Mileage Log Book

Employee ID :- _____ Name:- _____

Title :-_____ Dept:- _____

Vehicle Id _____ Signature:-_____

Date:	Time
Purpose:-	
Location - Origin	Destination
Odometer start	Odometer Finish
Gas fill up :- Yes/No	If yes Gallons filled
Cost per gallon	Amount paid
Paid Parking:-	Paid Tolls:-

Date:	Time
Purpose:-	
Location - Origin	Destination
Odometer start	Odometer Finish
Gas fill up :- Yes/No	If yes Gallons filled
Cost per gallon	Amount paid
Paid Parking:-	Paid Tolls:-

Mileage Log Book

Employee ID :- _____ Name:- _____

Title :-_____ Dept:- _____

Vehicle Id _____ Signature:-_____

Date: Time

Purpose:-

Location - Origin	Destination
Odometer start	Odometer Finish
Gas fill up :- Yes/No	If yes Gallons filled
Cost per gallon	Amount paid
Paid Parking:-	Paid Tolls:-

Date: Time

Purpose:-

Location - Origin	Destination
Odometer start	Odometer Finish
Gas fill up :- Yes/No	If yes Gallons filled
Cost per gallon	Amount paid
Paid Parking:-	Paid Tolls:-

Mileage Log Book

Employee ID :- _____ Name:- _____

Title :-_____ Dept:- _____

Vehicle Id _____ Signature:-_____

Date: | Time

Purpose:-

Location - Origin | Destination

Odometer start | Odometer Finish

Gas fill up :- Yes/No | If yes Gallons filled

Cost per gallon | Amount paid

Paid Parking:- | Paid Tolls:-

Date: | Time

Purpose:-

Location - Origin | Destination

Odometer start | Odometer Finish

Gas fill up :- Yes/No | If yes Gallons filled

Cost per gallon | Amount paid

Paid Parking:- | Paid Tolls:-

Mileage Log Book

Employee ID :- _____ Name:- _____

Title :-_____ Dept:- _____

Vehicle Id _____ Signature:-_____

Date:	Time
Purpose:-	
Location - Origin	Destination
Odometer start	Odometer Finish
Gas fill up :- Yes/No	If yes Gallons filled
Cost per gallon	Amount paid
Paid Parking:-	Paid Tolls:-

Date:	Time
Purpose:-	
Location - Origin	Destination
Odometer start	Odometer Finish
Gas fill up :- Yes/No	If yes Gallons filled
Cost per gallon	Amount paid
Paid Parking:-	Paid Tolls:-

Mileage Log Book

Employee ID :- _____ Name:- _____

Title :-_____ Dept:- _____

Vehicle Id _____ Signature:-_____

Date:	Time
Purpose:-	
Location - Origin	Destination
Odometer start	Odometer Finish
Gas fill up :- Yes/No	If yes Gallons filled
Cost per gallon	Amount paid
Paid Parking:-	Paid Tolls:-

Date:	Time
Purpose:-	
Location - Origin	Destination
Odometer start	Odometer Finish
Gas fill up :- Yes/No	If yes Gallons filled
Cost per gallon	Amount paid
Paid Parking:-	Paid Tolls:-

Mileage Log Book

Employee ID :- _____ Name:- _____

Title :-_____ Dept:- _____

Vehicle Id _____ Signature:-_____

Date: Time

Purpose:-

Location - Origin	Destination
Odometer start	Odometer Finish
Gas fill up :- Yes/No	If yes Gallons filled
Cost per gallon	Amount paid
Paid Parking:-	Paid Tolls:-

Date: Time

Purpose:-

Location - Origin	Destination
Odometer start	Odometer Finish
Gas fill up :- Yes/No	If yes Gallons filled
Cost per gallon	Amount paid
Paid Parking:-	Paid Tolls:-

Mileage Log Book

Employee ID :- _____ Name:- _____

Title :-_____ Dept:- _____

Vehicle Id _____ Signature:-_____

Date:	Time
Purpose:-	
Location - Origin	Destination
Odometer start	Odometer Finish
Gas fill up :- Yes/No	If yes Gallons filled
Cost per gallon	Amount paid
Paid Parking:-	Paid Tolls:-

Date:	Time
Purpose:-	
Location - Origin	Destination
Odometer start	Odometer Finish
Gas fill up :- Yes/No	If yes Gallons filled
Cost per gallon	Amount paid
Paid Parking:-	Paid Tolls:-

Mileage Log Book

Employee ID :- _____ Name:- _____

Title :- _____ Dept:- _____

Vehicle Id _____ Signature:- _____

Date:	Time
Purpose:-	
Location - Origin	Destination
Odometer start	Odometer Finish
Gas fill up :- Yes/No	If yes Gallons filled
Cost per gallon	Amount paid
Paid Parking:-	Paid Tolls:-

- -

Date:	Time
Purpose:-	
Location - Origin	Destination
Odometer start	Odometer Finish
Gas fill up :- Yes/No	If yes Gallons filled
Cost per gallon	Amount paid
Paid Parking:-	Paid Tolls:-

Mileage Log Book

Employee ID :- _____ Name:- _____

Title :-_____ Dept:- _____

Vehicle Id _____ Signature:-_____

Date:	Time
Purpose:-	
Location - Origin	Destination
Odometer start	Odometer Finish
Gas fill up :- Yes/No	If yes Gallons filled
Cost per gallon	Amount paid
Paid Parking:-	Paid Tolls:-

Date:	Time
Purpose:-	
Location - Origin	Destination
Odometer start	Odometer Finish
Gas fill up :- Yes/No	If yes Gallons filled
Cost per gallon	Amount paid
Paid Parking:-	Paid Tolls:-

Mileage Log Book

Employee ID :- _____ Name:- _____

Title :-_____ Dept:- _____

Vehicle Id _____ Signature:-_____

Date:	Time
Purpose:-	
Location - Origin	Destination
Odometer start	Odometer Finish
Gas fill up :- Yes/No	If yes Gallons filled
Cost per gallon	Amount paid
Paid Parking:-	Paid Tolls:-

Date:	Time
Purpose:-	
Location - Origin	Destination
Odometer start	Odometer Finish
Gas fill up :- Yes/No	If yes Gallons filled
Cost per gallon	Amount paid
Paid Parking:-	Paid Tolls:-

Mileage Log Book

Employee ID :- _____ Name:- _____

Title :- _____ Dept:- _____

Vehicle Id _____ Signature:- _____

Date:	Time
Purpose:-	
Location - Origin	Destination
Odometer start	Odometer Finish
Gas fill up :- Yes/No	If yes Gallons filled
Cost per gallon	Amount paid
Paid Parking:-	Paid Tolls:-

Date:	Time
Purpose:-	
Location - Origin	Destination
Odometer start	Odometer Finish
Gas fill up :- Yes/No	If yes Gallons filled
Cost per gallon	Amount paid
Paid Parking:-	Paid Tolls:-

Mileage Log Book

Employee ID :- _____ Name:- _____

Title :-_____ Dept:- _____

Vehicle Id _____ Signature:-_____

Date: Time

Purpose:-

Location - Origin	Destination
Odometer start	Odometer Finish
Gas fill up :- Yes/No	If yes Gallons filled
Cost per gallon	Amount paid
Paid Parking:-	Paid Tolls:-

Date: Time

Purpose:-

Location - Origin	Destination
Odometer start	Odometer Finish
Gas fill up :- Yes/No	If yes Gallons filled
Cost per gallon	Amount paid
Paid Parking:-	Paid Tolls:-

Mileage Log Book

Employee ID :- _____ Name:- _____

Title :-_____ Dept:- _____

Vehicle Id _____ Signature:-_____

Date:	Time
Purpose:-	
Location - Origin	Destination
Odometer start	Odometer Finish
Gas fill up :- Yes/No	If yes Gallons filled
Cost per gallon	Amount paid
Paid Parking:-	Paid Tolls:-

Date:	Time
Purpose:-	
Location - Origin	Destination
Odometer start	Odometer Finish
Gas fill up :- Yes/No	If yes Gallons filled
Cost per gallon	Amount paid
Paid Parking:-	Paid Tolls:-

Mileage Log Book

Employee ID :- _____ Name:- _____

Title :-_____ Dept:- _____

Vehicle Id _____ Signature:-_____

Date:	Time
Purpose:-	
Location - Origin	Destination
Odometer start	Odometer Finish
Gas fill up :- Yes/No	If yes Gallons filled
Cost per gallon	Amount paid
Paid Parking:-	Paid Tolls:-

Date:	Time
Purpose:-	
Location - Origin	Destination
Odometer start	Odometer Finish
Gas fill up :- Yes/No	If yes Gallons filled
Cost per gallon	Amount paid
Paid Parking:-	Paid Tolls:-

Mileage Log Book

Employee ID :- _____ Name:- _____

Title :-_____ Dept:- _____

Vehicle Id _____ Signature:-_____

Date:	Time
Purpose:-	
Location - Origin	Destination
Odometer start	Odometer Finish
Gas fill up :- Yes/No	If yes Gallons filled
Cost per gallon	Amount paid
Paid Parking:-	Paid Tolls:-

Date:	Time
Purpose:-	
Location - Origin	Destination
Odometer start	Odometer Finish
Gas fill up :- Yes/No	If yes Gallons filled
Cost per gallon	Amount paid
Paid Parking:-	Paid Tolls:-

Mileage Log Book

Employee ID :- _____ Name:- _____

Title :-_____ Dept:- _____

Vehicle Id _____ Signature:-_____

Date: Time

Purpose:-

Location - Origin	Destination
Odometer start	Odometer Finish
Gas fill up :- Yes/No	If yes Gallons filled
Cost per gallon	Amount paid
Paid Parking:-	Paid Tolls:-

Date: Time

Purpose:-

Location - Origin	Destination
Odometer start	Odometer Finish
Gas fill up :- Yes/No	If yes Gallons filled
Cost per gallon	Amount paid
Paid Parking:-	Paid Tolls:-

Mileage Log Book

Employee ID :- _____ Name:- _____

Title :-_____ Dept:- _____

Vehicle Id _____ Signature:-_____

Date:	Time
Purpose:-	
Location - Origin	Destination
Odometer start	Odometer Finish
Gas fill up :- Yes/No	If yes Gallons filled
Cost per gallon	Amount paid
Paid Parking:-	Paid Tolls:-

Date:	Time
Purpose:-	
Location - Origin	Destination
Odometer start	Odometer Finish
Gas fill up :- Yes/No	If yes Gallons filled
Cost per gallon	Amount paid
Paid Parking:-	Paid Tolls:-

Mileage Log Book

Employee ID :- _____ Name:- _____

Title :- _____ Dept:- _____

Vehicle Id _____ Signature:- _____

Date: Time

Purpose:-

Location - Origin	Destination
Odometer start	Odometer Finish
Gas fill up :- Yes/No	If yes Gallons filled
Cost per gallon	Amount paid
Paid Parking:-	Paid Tolls:-

Date: Time

Purpose:-

Location - Origin	Destination
Odometer start	Odometer Finish
Gas fill up :- Yes/No	If yes Gallons filled
Cost per gallon	Amount paid
Paid Parking:-	Paid Tolls:-

Mileage Log Book

Employee ID :- _____ Name:- _____

Title :-_____ Dept:- _____

Vehicle Id _____ Signature:-_____

Date:	Time
Purpose:-	
Location - Origin	Destination
Odometer start	Odometer Finish
Gas fill up :- Yes/No	If yes Gallons filled
Cost per gallon	Amount paid
Paid Parking:-	Paid Tolls:-

Date:	Time
Purpose:-	
Location - Origin	Destination
Odometer start	Odometer Finish
Gas fill up :- Yes/No	If yes Gallons filled
Cost per gallon	Amount paid
Paid Parking:-	Paid Tolls:-

Mileage Log Book

Employee ID :- _____ Name:- _____

Title :-_____ Dept:- _____

Vehicle Id _____ Signature:-_____

Date:	Time
Purpose:-	
Location - Origin	Destination
Odometer start	Odometer Finish
Gas fill up :- Yes/No	If yes Gallons filled
Cost per gallon	Amount paid
Paid Parking:-	Paid Tolls:-

Date:	Time
Purpose:-	
Location - Origin	Destination
Odometer start	Odometer Finish
Gas fill up :- Yes/No	If yes Gallons filled
Cost per gallon	Amount paid
Paid Parking:-	Paid Tolls:-

Mileage Log Book

Employee ID :- _____ Name:- _____

Title :-_____ Dept:- _____

Vehicle Id _____ Signature:-_____

Date:	Time
Purpose:-	
Location - Origin	Destination
Odometer start	Odometer Finish
Gas fill up :- Yes/No	If yes Gallons filled
Cost per gallon	Amount paid
Paid Parking:-	Paid Tolls:-

Date:	Time
Purpose:-	
Location - Origin	Destination
Odometer start	Odometer Finish
Gas fill up :- Yes/No	If yes Gallons filled
Cost per gallon	Amount paid
Paid Parking:-	Paid Tolls:-

Mileage Log Book

Employee ID :- _____ Name:- _____

Title :-_____ Dept:- _____

Vehicle Id _____ Signature:-_____

Date:	Time
Purpose:-	
Location - Origin	Destination
Odometer start	Odometer Finish
Gas fill up :- Yes/No	If yes Gallons filled
Cost per gallon	Amount paid
Paid Parking:-	Paid Tolls:-

Date:	Time
Purpose:-	
Location - Origin	Destination
Odometer start	Odometer Finish
Gas fill up :- Yes/No	If yes Gallons filled
Cost per gallon	Amount paid
Paid Parking:-	Paid Tolls:-

Mileage Log Book

Employee ID :- _____ Name:- _____

Title :-_____ Dept:- _____

Vehicle Id _____ Signature:-_____

Date:	Time
Purpose:-	
Location - Origin	Destination
Odometer start	Odometer Finish
Gas fill up :- Yes/No	If yes Gallons filled
Cost per gallon	Amount paid
Paid Parking:-	Paid Tolls:-

Date:	Time
Purpose:-	
Location - Origin	Destination
Odometer start	Odometer Finish
Gas fill up :- Yes/No	If yes Gallons filled
Cost per gallon	Amount paid
Paid Parking:-	Paid Tolls:-

Mileage Log Book

Employee ID :- _____ Name:- _____

Title :-_____ Dept:- _____

Vehicle Id _____ Signature:-_____

Date: _____ Time _____

Purpose:- _____

Location - Origin	Destination
Odometer start	Odometer Finish
Gas fill up :- Yes/No	If yes Gallons filled
Cost per gallon	Amount paid
Paid Parking:-	Paid Tolls:-

Date: _____ Time _____

Purpose:- _____

Location - Origin	Destination
Odometer start	Odometer Finish
Gas fill up :- Yes/No	If yes Gallons filled
Cost per gallon	Amount paid
Paid Parking:-	Paid Tolls:-

Mileage Log Book

Employee ID :- _____ Name:- _____

Title :- _____ Dept:- _____

Vehicle Id _____ Signature:- _____

Date:	Time
Purpose:-	
Location - Origin	Destination
Odometer start	Odometer Finish
Gas fill up :- Yes/No	If yes Gallons filled
Cost per gallon	Amount paid
Paid Parking:-	Paid Tolls:-

Date:	Time
Purpose:-	
Location - Origin	Destination
Odometer start	Odometer Finish
Gas fill up :- Yes/No	If yes Gallons filled
Cost per gallon	Amount paid
Paid Parking:-	Paid Tolls:-

www.ingramcontent.com/pod-product-compliance
Lightning Source LLC
Chambersburg PA
CBHW030647220526
45463CB00005B/1668